T0268500

Cats and Kittens

FIRST EDITION

Senior Editor Carrie Love; **US Senior Editor** Shannon Beatty; **Project Editor** Kritika Gupta;
Editor Sophie Parkes; **Assistant Editor** Gunjan Mewati; **Project Art Editor** Polly Appleton;
Art Editor Mohd Zishan; **Assistant Art Editors** Bhagyashree Nayak, Simran Lakhiani;
Jacket Coordinator Issy Walsh; **Jacket Designer** Debangshi Basu;
DTP Designers Dheeraj Singh, Nityanand Kumar; **Picture Researcher** Rituraj Singher Singh;
Senior Production Editor Jennifer Murray; **Production Controller** Basia Ossowska;
Managing Editors Penny Smith, Monica Saigal; **Managing Art Editors** Mabel Chan, Ivy Sengupta;
Delhi Team Head Malavika Talukder; **Publishing Manager** Francesca Youngr Young;
Creative Director Helen Senior; **Publishing Director** Sarah Larter;
Reading Consultant Dr. Barbara Marinak; **Subject Consultant** Bruce Fogle MBE DVM MRCVS

THIS EDITION

Editorial Management by Oriel Square
Produced for DK by WonderLab Group LLC
Jennifer Emmett, Erica Green, Kate Hale, *Founders*

Editors Grace Hill Smith, Libby Romero, Michaela Weglinski;
Photography Editors Kelley Miller, Annette Kiesow, Nicole DiMella;
Managing Editor Rachel Houghton; **Designers** Project Design Company; **Researcher** Michelle Harris;
Copy Editor Lori Merritt; **Indexer** Connie Binder; **Proofreader** Larry Shea;
Reading Specialist Dr. Jennifer Albro; **Curriculum Specialist** Elaine Larson

Published in the United States by DK Publishing
1745 Broadway, 20th Floor, New York, NY 10019
Copyright © 2023 Dorling Kindersley Limited
DK, a Division of Penguin Random House LLC
22 23 24 25 26 10 9 8 7 6 5 4 3 2 1
001–333855–May/2023

A catalog record for this book
is available from the Library of Congress.
HC ISBN: 978-0-7440-7101-6
PB ISBN: 978-0-7440-7102-3

DK books are available at special discounts when purchased in bulk for sales promotions, premiums,
fundraising, or educational use. For details, contact: DK Publishing Special Markets,
1745 Broadway, 20th Floor, New York, NY 10019
SpecialSales@dk.com

Printed and bound in China

The publisher would like to thank the following for their kind permission to reproduce their images:
a=above; c=center; b=below; l=left; r=right; t=top; b/g=background

Shutterstock.com: Anurak Pongpatimet 20–21

Cover images: *Front:* **Shutterstock.com:** Ollivka; *Back:* **Shutterstock.com:** D–sign Studio 10 cla, miniwide cra, bl

All other images © Dorling Kindersley
For more information see: www.dkimages.com

For the curious
www.dk.com

Level

2

Cats and Kittens

Caryn Jenner

Contents

6   Let's Meet Cats

12   Types of Cats

14   Parts of a Cat

16   Kittens

22 Fun with Cats

30 Glossary

31 Index

32 Quiz

Let's Meet Cats

Purr, purr. Meow, meow. What's that? It's a cat, of course!

There are more than 500 million cats around the world. That's a lot! Cats are one of the most popular pets in the world.

Cats first started living with people around 5,000 years ago.

Meow!

ginger cat

tabby cat

Cats are covered in soft fur. Their fur can be different colors and patterns. Cats have sharp claws and teeth.

tortoiseshell cat

black-and-white cat

colorpoint cat

They have pointed ears and bright eyes. Cats have thin, wiry whiskers that stick out around small noses and have long tails.

A cat that is angry or scared hisses and arches its back. Its fur stands on end to make it look bigger.
Sometimes, its ears lie flat against its head, too.

Cats rub their heads against people to show their affection.

A happy cat purrs. It might also push its claws in and out or rub its face against its special human.

Types of Cats

Different cat breeds are different sizes. Many cats are a mix of breeds.

Siamese

Abyssinian

Persian

Maine Coon

European Shorthair

Parts of a Cat

Find out more about the special features of a cat.

A cat has keen eyes that can see in the dark.

A cat's whiskers act as feelers, helping it detect objects.

Tiny spikes on a cat's tongue help with grooming and lapping up water.

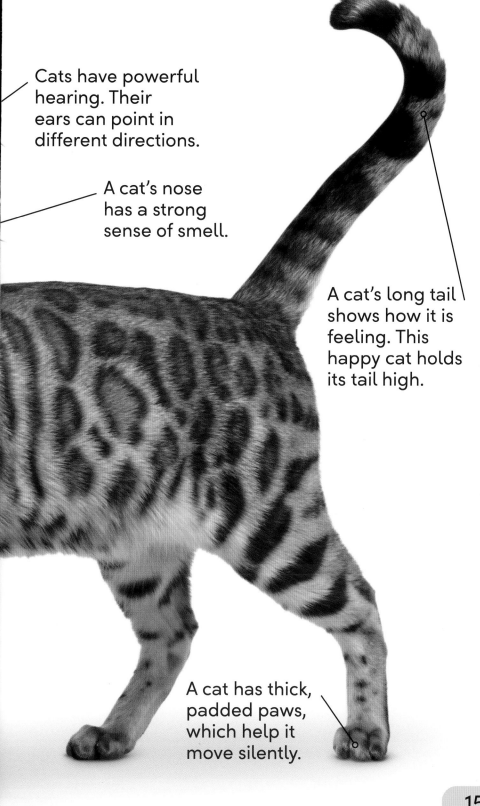

Cats have powerful hearing. Their ears can point in different directions.

A cat's nose has a strong sense of smell.

A cat's long tail shows how it is feeling. This happy cat holds its tail high.

A cat has thick, padded paws, which help it move silently.

Kittens

A mother cat gives birth to a litter of kittens. There can be as many as 10 kittens in a litter!

Usually, there are only four to six kittens. The kittens stay near their mother to keep warm. They feed on her milk.

Purr...

Newborn kittens often purr while feeding.

newborn kitten

A newborn kitten is so small that it can lie in your hand. Newborn kittens can't see or hear.

Newborn kittens snuggle together to stay warm.

Their eyes and ears will open at about 2 weeks old.
At about 3 weeks old, kittens start walking.

Soon, kittens learn to run and jump and play. They also get used to being around humans.

Kittens should stay with their mother until they are about 10 weeks old.

Always be gentle with cats and kittens.

mother with her kitten

Fun with Cats

Cats love to play. It's good exercise. They like to run and climb. They like to hide and roll around.

Sometimes, cats pretend they are hunting. They chase toys and pounce on them! Sometimes, they hunt for real and catch birds and mice.

This cat chases a red ball.

A cat's tail helps it to balance. That's how cats walk in tricky places such as the top of a fence.

A cat's special muscles mean it can twist around, so it usually lands on its feet. Maybe that's why people say that cats have nine lives!

Cats walk on their toes. This helps them to balance.

Cats stay clean by grooming themselves. They lick their fur and paws, which keeps them cool. Sometimes cats groom each other.

Cats keep their claws trimmed by scratching. When they're outdoors, they scratch on trees and fences.

Cats spend most of their day sleeping. They might sleep curled up in a ball or stretched out in the sun. Cats often take quick catnaps.

Cats spend two-thirds of their lives sleeping!

Sometimes, their tails and ears twitch when they sleep. Do you think these cats are dreaming?

Glossary

Cat
A warm-blooded animal with soft fur, a small nose, and claws that can retract

Breed
A group of cats that all have the same special features

Groom
An action that an animal takes to keep its coat clean and tidy

Kitten
A young cat that is not yet fully grown

Pounce
An action that an animal takes when it swoops in or jumps on something

Wiry
Something that is stiff but flexible, like a piece of wire

Index

angry cats 10

breeds 12

claws 8, 11, 26

ears 9, 10, 15, 19, 29

eyes 9, 14, 19

fur 8, 10, 26

grooming 14, 26

happy cats 11, 15

hunting 22

kittens 16–21

noses 9, 15

parts of cats 14–15

paws 15, 26

playing 20, 22, 23

pounce 22

purring 6, 11, 17

scared cats 10

sleeping 28–29

tails 9, 15, 24, 29

tongue 14

whiskers 9, 14

Quiz

Answer the questions to see what you have learned. Check your answers in the key below.

1. About how many cats are there in the world?

2. Why might a cat hiss and arch its back?

3. What do a cat's whiskers do?

4. About how old are kittens when their eyes and ears open?

5. How much of their lives do cats spend sleeping?

1. More than 500 million 2. If it is angry or scared
3. They act as feelers, helping to detect objects
4. Two weeks old 5. Two-thirds of their lives